I CAN ONLY DRAW WORMS

by Will Mabbitt

To
THE GRAMMAR
SCHOOL AT
LEEDS

best wishes

Will
Mabbitt

This book is about worms.

(I can only draw worms.)

Here's worm **ONE.**

Here's worm **TWO**.

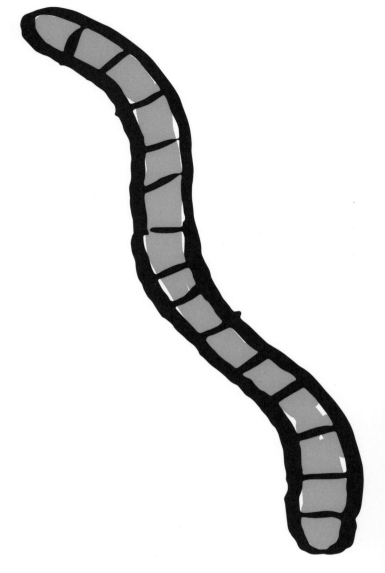

Here they are both together.
It's hard to know which is which.

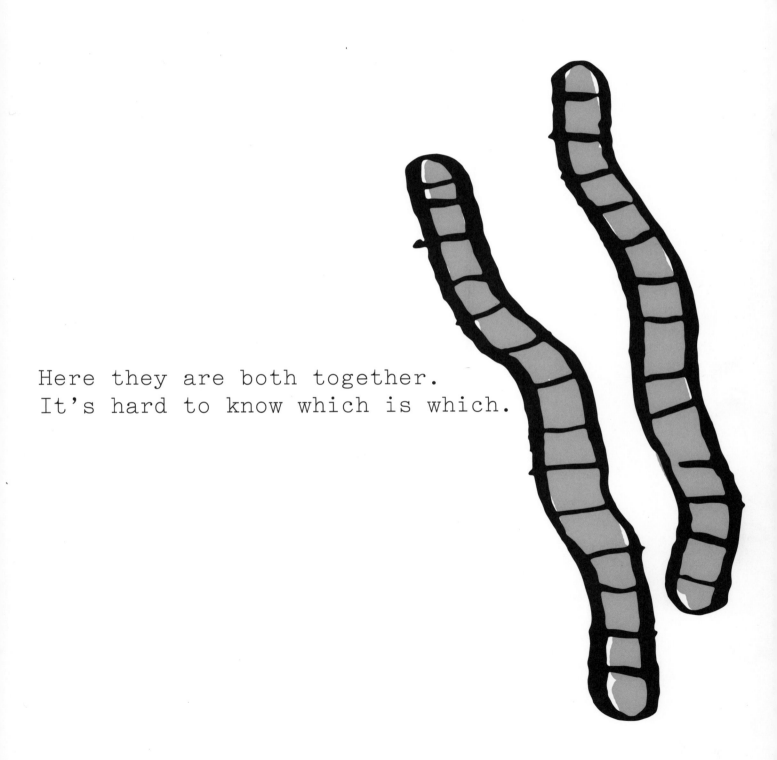

I'll give the second worm glasses.

That's better.

Now you can tell them apart.

Here's worm **THREE.**

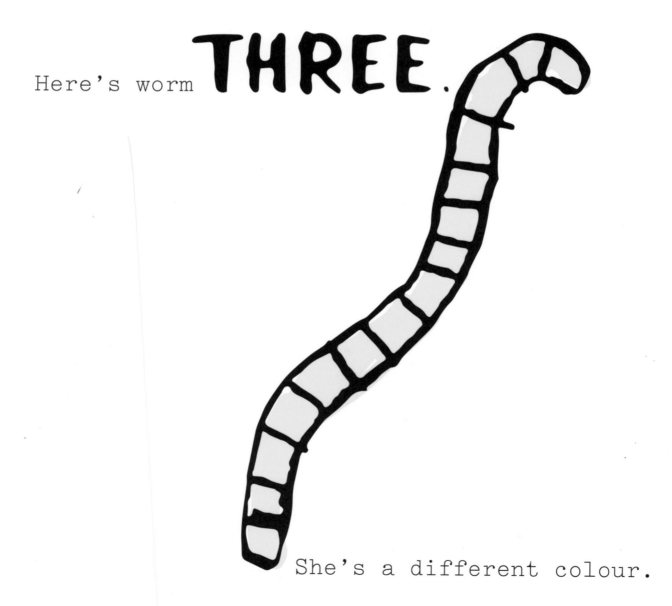

She's a different colour.

No reason — I just lost my pen.

Hello, worm **FOUR**.
Worm FOUR thinks he's in
charge of all the other worms.

I don't know why.

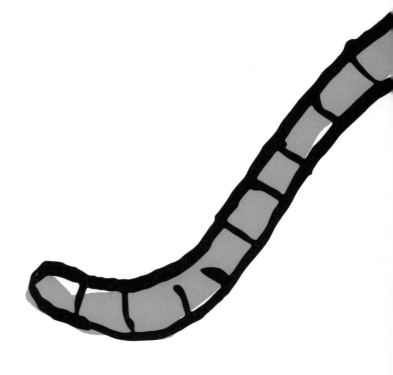

Here's worm **FIVE**.
He's a little poorly, I'm afraid.
Poorly worms look just like
normal worms.

The next page is really exciting.
Worm SIX is riding on a flying unicorn!

I can't draw flying unicorns.

I've drawn worm FIVE again instead.

Worm **SIX** flies his unicorn
all the way to meet worm SEVEN
who lives in `outer space!`

On the way worm SIX has an `amazing adventure!`

We'll skip all that.

Here's a picture of
him meeting worm SEVEN.

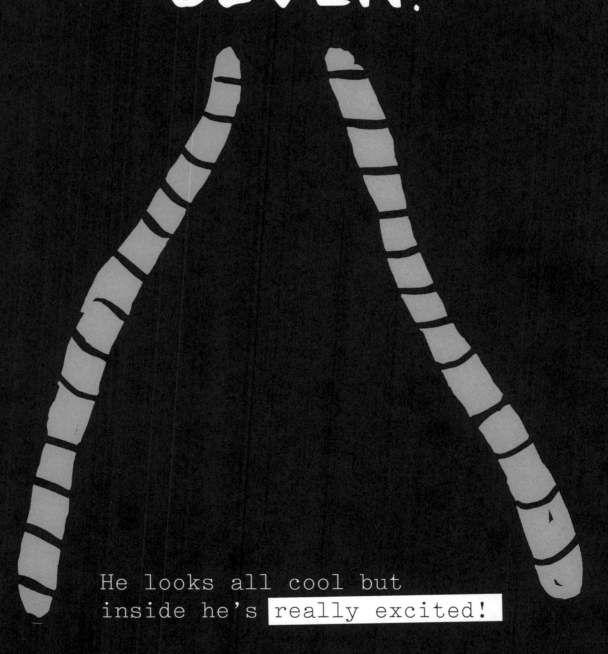

He looks all cool but
inside he's really excited!

OH DEAR!

THERE'S BEEN A DRE

ADFUL ACCIDENT.

It's **not true** that if a worm is cut in half it makes two worms.

It makes **two half worms.**

Here's worm
EIGHT.

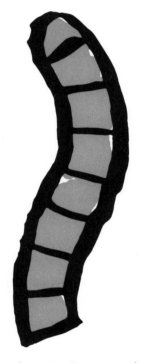

And here's worm

EIGHT-AND-A-HALF.

This page is blank.
Worm NINE is MISSING.

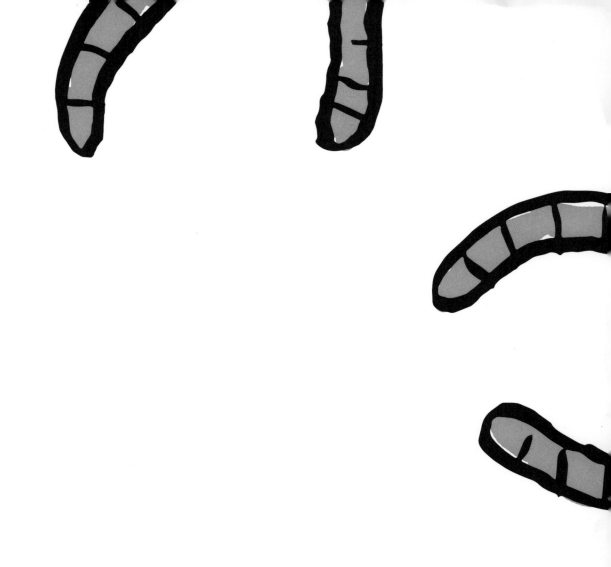

And the others are starting to get worried.

Here's worm **TEN** instead. The last worm.
He looks the same as worm ONE.

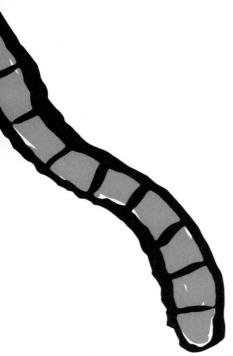

Oh! It is worm ONE.

Here's worm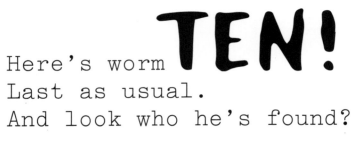
Last as usual.
And look who he's found?

Worm **NINE!**
He'd just nipped to the toilet.

That's OK, worm NINE.
Everybody has to go sometimes.

So now that's . . .

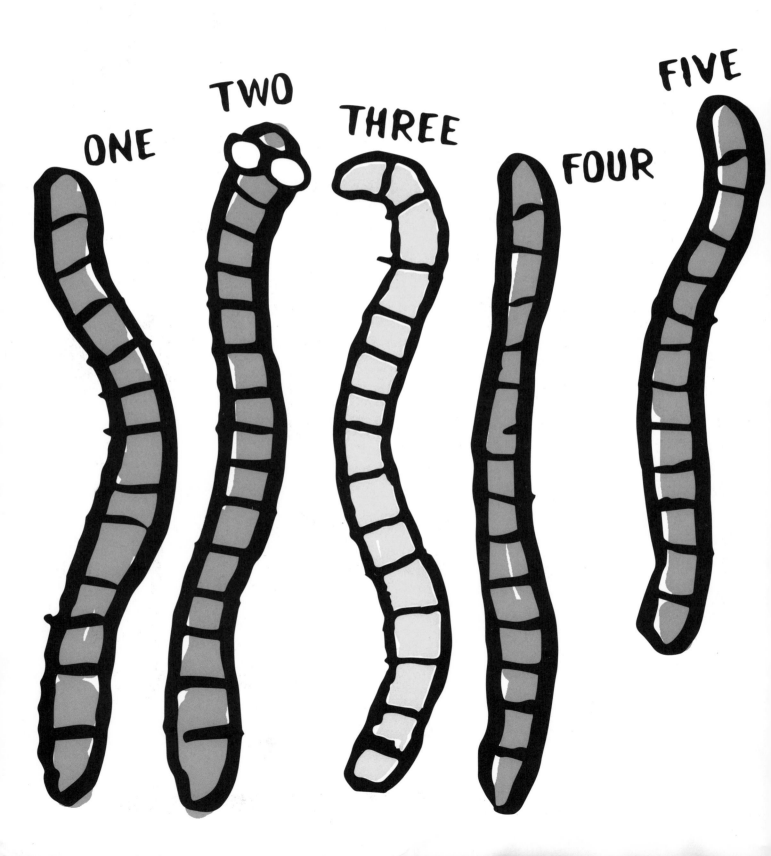

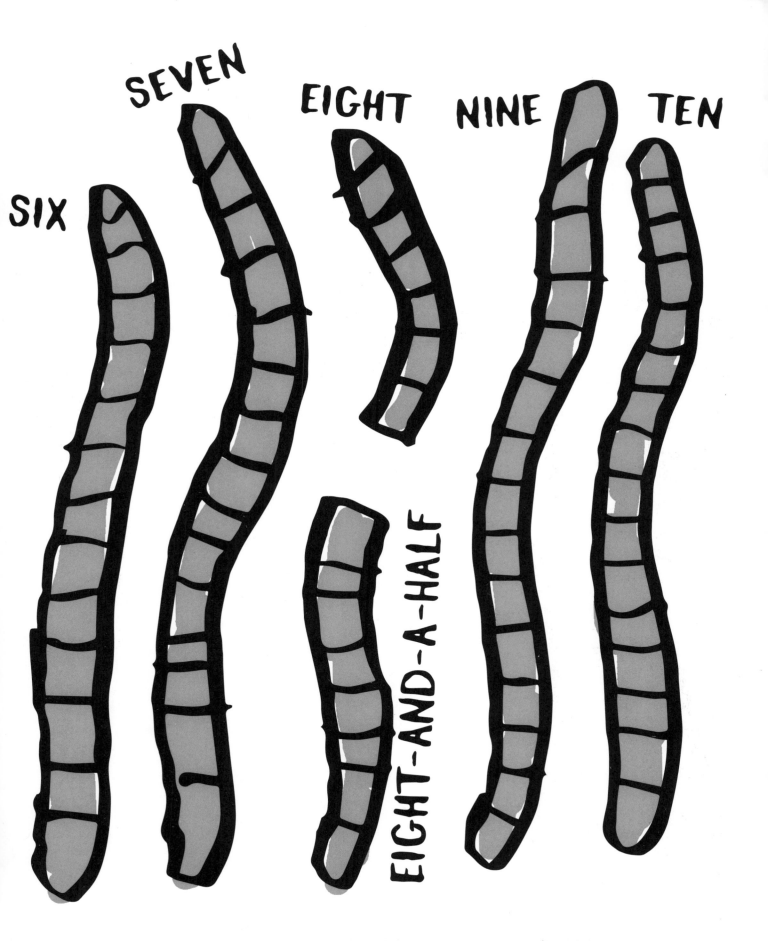

Ten worms. All friends together.

This book was about worms.

(I can only draw worms.)

For Zero — who should be at the
start of every counting book.

PUFFIN BOOKS

UK | USA | Canada | Ireland | Australia
India | New Zealand | South Africa

Puffin Books is part of the Penguin Random House group of companies
whose addresses can be found at global.penguinrandomhouse.com.

www.penguin.co.uk
www.puffin.co.uk
www.ladybird.co.uk

 Penguin
Random House
UK

First published 2017

005

The moral right of the author and illustrator has been asserted

Printed in Italy

A CIP catalogue record for this book is available from the British Library

ISBN: 978–0–141–37518-2

All correspondence to:
Puffin Books
Penguin Random House Children's
80 Strand, London WC2R 0RL